MW00561257

Table of Contents

Forward

What showed me the need for clarity in medical charting? My first faculty residency position.

Teaching attending supervision requires that faculty routinely sign off on their residents' charts. When I began reviewing them, I was appalled. If it hadn't been for their verbal presentations and discussions, I wouldn't have recognized many of these patients by their respective charts. On average, my residents could not effectively write to convey the patient's story, nor could they write their own thought processes clearly.

Why not? My residents were intelligent and well educated. Most graduated from top universities and medical schools. Some of them had earned multiple graduate degrees. Many were fluent in multiple languages. These were among the brightest people around. This should have been a simple task for them. Why couldn't they write up their patients' stories or their own thinking, clearly, accurately and succinctly?

Were my residents simply working their way through a long checklist? Were they plugging away, mindlessly inputting data, like machines? Perhaps there was no respect for what a medical chart can do. Maybe charting was just another mundane, time-consuming, administrative duty.

Initially, I was disappointed. Then, I realized the culprit: *No one had formally taught them medical charting.* They lacked instruction.

The true nature of the problem only emerged when I decided to create a short written guideline. I realized that I too had received little formal training in charting. Was there a lapse in our education, a glitch that affected only two groups: my own fellow residents and this particular group that I supervised? That would be highly unlikely, but possible. I asked my colleagues and fellow faculty members. They, too, had received little formal education in charting.

Since it was not limited to an occasional oversight, *the problem seemed systemic:*

> *Physicians tended to receive little formal education in medical charting.*

To assist my residents, I wrote a 2-page handout. I included insights gleaned from my anecdotal experience and little bit of training. I tried to explain the why's of charting with the how's. I distributed it to my residents and fellow faculty. Having done my part, I would move on to other projects.

Or so I thought. Since those days, I've had ample opportunity to view my colleagues' charts from diverse specialties across a wide range of training and clinical experience. Many reflected the problems I had noted with my own residents. My impression of a pervasive lack of clarity was further confirmed when I reviewed charts as an expert medical witness. I then began to examine virtually all charts from my rudimentary medico-legal perspective. Again, I found a wide spectrum in quality.

Two questions kept coming back: *What could improve or create consistent quality in medical charting? What resources are available to help physicians?*

In emergency medicine (my specialty), many departments require charting classes for coding and billing. While the training is helpful, the sessions primarily benefit the larger, corporate structure of a medical group or hospital, and not the individual physician. Unless you are a solo practitioner or partner in a small, democratic group with little overhead, you're unlikely to see a direct, a 1:1 benefit in improved charting.

Other than that, there were no classes, no training, and no book or handbook. The closest things to a resource were books and seminars about expert witnessing, but they only peripherally touched on issues of effective charting.

The problem remained, and trying to address it became the genesis of this handbook.

Introduction

Charting is an essential part of modern medical practice. How can physicians make effective 'next-step' decisions for their patients, if they are not sure what happened, or why?

More to the point: *How can physicians be expected to chart well and chart effectively, if no formal training has been provided?*

Part of the problem is the nature of the task and a physician's time constraints. Charting is writing, pure and simple. But writers in other fields have the opportunity to revise multiple drafts and put the piece aside from time to time. Even professional writers use editors to help with grammar, punctuation, consistency and clarity.

In clinical medicine, we typically do not have someone else look at our medical charting in detail before submitting it. Even in clinical training programs, supervising physicians are often too busy to routinely give thorough feedback on a trainee's written work. Physicians themselves do not normally have the luxury of employing editors or multiple drafts. Even when we are careful and thoughtful, mistakes are bound to happen.

Physicians with charting systems, including real-time scribes or similar staff to transcribe their dictations, have an advantage. By seeing whether their vision matches what their scribes have charted, these physicians act primarily as editors, and not as authors. But this service is generally unavailable for most residents or medical students.

Most clinicians learn to chart well enough through years of trial and error, but this is an inefficient process. More times than I care to remember, for instance, I've seen charts with:
- Inconsistencies,
- Boilerplate language that describes things that may or may not have been done, and
- Language that does not tell a complete story of what happened and why.

Certain types of errors can be easily avoided, if physicians were given clear, formal guidance.

Formal charting education would benefit physicians as well as healthcare institutions. An excellent charting course with special emphasis on writing and some of the legal functions of a medical chart can primarily benefit the physician, because:
- Better charting leads to improved written communication between physicians,

- Better communication leads to improved patient care and resource utilization, and
- Better resource utilization leads to liberating physicians' time for other tasks.

The corporate structure of the medical group and hospital can benefit, secondarily, in several ways from:

- Decreased litigation,
- Decreased physician stress,
- Decreased physician burnout, and
- Increased physician productivity.

Better charting benefits everyone.

Better charting is the purpose of this handbook. I made it brief, because your time is valuable. I tried to balance brevity with completeness, and I included examples that I hope will be useful.

This handbook is intended to guide those who are just starting to develop their clinical writing skills: students and residents. However, even experienced attendings could find material useful in their clinical practice.

The Medical Chart's Three Functions

A medical chart serves 3 basic functions:
1. A basis for billing.
2. A form for transferring clinical information.
3. A legal document, describing events that occurred.

The Medical Chart as a Bill

While the medical chart as a form for transferring patient information is clearly its most important function for physicians, its significance as a bill in today's healthcare economy cannot be underestimated.

The chart demonstrates the amount of medical work the patient received. We are able to bill for our services if and only if we put it in the chart. Early in my clinical rotations as a 3rd year medical student, an attending or senior resident told me:

If something wasn't charted, it wasn't done.

Like an auto mechanic who gives a customer an itemized bill for an oil change, oil filter replacement, and labor, the medical chart acts as list of examinations, parts and services.

You will encounter many resources and training opportunities to help your charting as a form of billing. As such, we only discuss it briefly in this handbook.

The Medical Chart as a Form of Transferring Clinical Information

Although patients can tell you a lot, there is a lot of information they cannot tell you. This is especially true for physicians' thought processes that lead to a diagnosis or plan. The chart is a form of communication.

Ideally, your communication should be clear and organized. Unclear and disorganized charting can be detrimental for patient care. Keep in mind that your colleagues need to know:

- What happened,
- What you were thinking, and
- Why you did what you did.

Charting may initially seem to be time-consuming, but the opposite is true. Reading the chart and then verifying the history and physical can be more efficient than re-doing both the history and physical from scratch.

The Medical Chart as a Legal Document

In the same way that the chart is a bill, it is also a legal document. Your chart is one record of events that occurred. If there is ever a question as to what happened and why, the chart will be a primary resource. In many instances, the chart will be a central piece of evidence.

Many people may review your chart, including quality control staff, attorneys, expert witnesses, the judge and the jury.

To Chart Effectively, Write Effectively

As an emergency physician, my charts typically consist of patients' histories, physicals, initial assessments, and initial plans. In many instances, there are brief progress and procedure notes.

The same lessons for writing good, clear, concise emergency medicine charting apply to all charting, because the same concepts for effective charting persist across specialties. Clear communication is universal. Good, clear, concise charting comes from good, clear, concise writing.

Why It's Necessary to Rethink Writing

CONTEXT: Most physicians once gained extensive writing experience in grade school, high school and college. Those who went on to graduate school most likely had to write even more. Along the way, there were book reports, 5-paragraph essays, term papers and graduate theses. Once medical school started, physicians received little, if any, formal writing practice. We put many of those hard-earned skills away. Years pass; the writing skills acquired through previous training can atrophy. As healthcare providers, we now face the challenge of writing virtually every time we're on duty. Writing is part of our jobs. *But how often do we think about what we are doing, as writers?* This section is designed to help us think about writing in a different way, and in the process, acquire enhanced writing skills.

Stephen King, the award-winning novelist, says, "You must not come lightly to the blank page."[1(p.106)] How much more seriously should we be, writing a document that is a bill, a legal document and a patient care resource, all at once?

Take writing seriously while charting. Before we can do this, we should first think about what writing is.

What is Writing?
Stephen King suggests that writing is telepathy.[1(p.106)] Through writing, the author and reader attempt to share the same thoughts on a subject. Psycholinguist Stephen Pinker uses the analogy of a writer as a cinematographer, directing the reader's perspective with words in the same way that a cinematographer uses camera angles and scene cuts to tell a story.[2(Ch.1)]

The Goal of Writing
If the reader understands the author's thoughts
in the way that the author intended,
then the author has succeeded.

Good writing does not fit a single formula,[2 (Ch.1)] but it achieves the same end. You've seen examples of good writing in medical charts, research, news articles, op-eds, novels and even textbooks. While certain general concepts permeate good writing, different authors can wield the same concepts differently. There are as many ways to write as there are authors.

Implications for Medical Charting
As you chart, you become a writer. In your mind as a writer, you have a vision of the patient that you have collected through your history, examination, and analysis. One of your goals is to transfer this vision into the reader's mind in order to make the reader see what you see. How well you use your words translates into how well you project your thoughts. How clearly you project your thoughts determines the picture of your patient in the reader's mind.

But how do you draw this picture? How do you place your vision into the reader's mind? And how do you do this with just words, when there are so many details?

Manage the Story
Start with a clear concept of what you are trying to communicate.[2(Ch.2)] Know the story you are trying to tell before you tell it. This is like having a topic sentence.

Without knowing in advance what you want to describe, your charting will lack focus, and the patient's story will meander. In other words, *beware of charting before you have at least a rough idea of what is going on with your patient.* Even a brief history can meander and get lost. Your reader will be distracted and may have to read your chart multiple times.

Reading the same piece of writing several times takes up time and energy. Both time and energy are in limited supply. Keep your vision of your patient in mind.

Manage the Details
The classic text on writing, Strunk's *The Elements of Style,* gives us some guidance about managing the details:

> *It is not that every detail is given; that would be impossible, as well as to no purpose; but that all the significant details are given, and not vaguely, but with such definitiveness that the reader, in imagination, can project himself into the scene.*[3(p.22)]

Stephen King describes it another way, telling us that a good description consists of a few carefully selected details that stand for everything else.[1(p.173)]

Too Much
One temptation might be to write everything, thinking that a full documentation of background information

and your actions would be intelligible to anyone. After all, your chart's audience may come to include:

- Members of your specialty,
- Members of other specialties,
- Nurses,
- Physical therapists,
- Billing staff,
- Insurance company auditors,
- Attorneys, paralegals, judges, and
- Members of a jury.

However, even if your chart ends up among a non-medical audience, such as in legal proceedings, a physician will often interpret it for the others. Therefore, keep in mind your immediate audience: *other medical professionals.*

Knowing what to describe and what to leave out is important to telling a story.

- Sparse description leaves your reader bewildered;
- Over-description buries your reader in details.[1(p.174)]

A thoughtful choice of both the positives and negatives in a review of systems will help draw the vision of your patient's story, but if you list every detail that the patient tells you, your reader can lose focus on your vision. For example, describing the details of a patient's chronic arthritis and carpal tunnel syndrome when her primary complaint is abdominal pain suspicious for an acute bowel obstruction may likely get in the way of drawing a clear picture.

To help you manage the information to include in your charting, ask yourself:
Does the information:
- *Drive your story forward, or*
- *Leave it mired in the details?*

If it's the latter, then leave it out.

Too Little
An important concept to keep in mind as you chart is what Pinker calls the 'Curse of Knowledge'.[2(Ch.3)] The Curse of Knowledge is the difficulty imagining the viewpoint of someone who doesn't know what you know.[2(Ch.3)]

Often, the writer overestimates how much the reader knows about the subject or an event. Writing notes to yourself to jog your memory of patient interaction is very different than trying to provide the necessary details for another to recreate your vision, for instance. The writer's Curse of Knowledge leaves readers filling in the blanks with information they may not have.[2(Ch.3)] Keep in mind who your audience is likely to be and what their needs are, because:

> *Charting is <u>not</u> writing notes to yourself about your patient.*
> *Charting <u>is</u> writing essential content for other people to use when you're not there.*

The Curse of Knowledge is the primary reason that good professionals write bad prose.[2(Ch.3)]

Related to the Curse of Knowledge is the delicate balance of the degree of abstraction that a writer can effectively use.[2(Ch.3)] The more sophisticated your audience is about the particular subject, the less you need to spell out the connections.[2(Ch.3)] You should write differently if you were describing a patient's case to a non-medical audience than the same case to a medical audience. At the same time, if you incorrectly assume that your readers know too much or too little, they will likely get lost. Even experts in a subject may become confused, lost or bored if too many elementary connections are spelled out.[2(Ch.3)] More importantly, you are not communicating effectively.

In general:

> *Write your chart with the intention of communicating with another physician.*

Other physicians will be your most frequent audience, but when in doubt, assume the audience knows just a little less rather than a little more.[2(Ch.5)]

Charting in Three Forms:

Writing A Billing Document

As a general principle, the more work you demonstrate, the more you can bill. Complex patient encounters need more work done, and can be billed more. Simpler patient encounters need less work, and can be billed less.

Work can be both physical and intellectual:

Physical:
1. I placed an 18 gauge IV in the right antecubital fossa.
2. I obtained an arterial blood gas from the left, radial artery.
3. I applied a thumb spica splint to the left wrist.

Intellectual:
1. I performed a 10-organ system review of systems and it is negative except for [x].
2. I interpreted the EKG and it shows [x].
3. My read of the chest x-ray shows [x].

Complex cases will require mental work, including consulting with colleagues.

Further nuances regarding the chart as a billing document are beyond the scope of this text. Since other resources cover this material, our discussion on it has been brief.

The important, general concept is this:
If you demonstrate more of your work, you can bill more.

Writing A Medical Document

CONTEXT: Most other medical writing is for research and grants, and there is ample guidance for these. However, little guidance exists for clarity in clinical documentation.

Medical Writing

Medical charting is a type of technical writing. It has its own style and form. The beginning and end of the chart are typically prose. Sometimes, they are the only opportunities you will have to tell the patient's story clearly and in your own words. Many times, the middle of the chart is a form with circles, slashes, check boxes, and drop down menus to complete. These forms do not convey a clear story, although they are great data capture for billing.

A Different Kind of Prose

Medical charting differs from other prose in form. The classic for essay writing, *Elements of Style,* instructs that the topic sentence comes at the beginning, succeeding sentences develop the statement made by the topic sentence, and the final sentence should either emphasize the topic sentence or note an important consequence.[3(p.17)]

In a medical chart, we do not start with a topic sentence to frame the rest of the discussion.

Medical charts start more like a story told from beginning to end. We do not start a traditional written (or oral) history and physical with a statement like, "I believe this patient has a CHF exacerbation." Instead, the story unfolds relatively chronologically. Keeping your conclusion in mind is useful as you tell the patient's story because it will focus your charting. You will be less likely to run off on unnecessary tangents.

While charting is a form a storytelling, be clear about its function: conveying information instead of creative writing. A chart is not a place to build suspense. This is not the place to recreate a medical drama, however exciting or challenging your shift may have been. Keep to true to the patient's story and needs.

Note that your charting style may be different from your colleague's, but it should achieve the same goal:
Telling the patient's story in a clear,
complete, and concise way.

To do so requires that we understand how sentences, syntax, voice and words work. These are our tools. We must use them effectively.

Sentences and Syntax

The beginnings and ends of medical charts are brief, compared with the prose of most other writers. However in just a few sentences, physicians have to pack in a lot of information. Knowing how to use sentences effectively is essential.

Sentences

So what is a sentence? A string of words? A string of words with a subject and a predicate? In *How to Write a Sentence and How to Read One,* Stanley Fish defines a sentence as an organization of items in the world and a structure of logical relationships.[4(Ch.2)]

A sentence is about organization and logic. Sentences anchor connections for words in a greater structure. Without sentences, words and the concepts that words stand for are left hanging in a void.

It takes skill to produce a sentence. The skill of linking events, actions and objects in a strict logic is also the skill of creating a world.[4(Ch.4)] In some regards, creating a world echoes Pinker's idea of the writer as a cinematographer.[2(Ch.1)] But just like a cinematographer, remember to have your whole vision of the patient's situation in mind before beginning. You cannot produce a logical sequence of events without knowing the destination.

Goal of A Sentence
The goal in writing a sentence is not to say everything that you could possibly say about a topic.[4(Ch.4)] If that were the case, no one would ever finish a sentence.[4(Ch.4)] The goal is to communicate your perspective clearly and well.[4(Ch.4)] In other words, write the relevant parts and then move on.

A Good Sentence
For writers to transplant their vision into the reader's mind, the sentences must be well constructed. But how do we construct good sentences?

Keep sentence structure simple.

It's too easy to get tangled in complex rhetoric. Communication breaks down, and the vision that the author tries to project into the reader's mind becomes blurry.

Syntax and Syntactic trees

To further understand how sentences become tangled, we will examine how groups of phrases come together grammatically (syntax).

Psycholinguists use the metaphor of a tree to describe syntax.[2(Ch.4)] Syntax is a language's grammatical structure. Syntax is how a series of phrases come together to organize ideas in a string of words.[2(Ch.4)] A tree is a metaphor for how smaller phrases embed into larger phrases.[2(Ch.4)] Each branch is a phrase. In written language, readers use the arrangements of words and phrases to recover the relationships between the ideas in the author's mind.[2(Ch.4)]

Syntax trees branch to the right, to the left and in the middle.

Right branching trees tend to be easier to understand.[2(Ch.4)] Right branching trees place the most complicated phrases at the end of the sentence. English is naturally a right branching language.[2(Ch.4)]

Examples of right branching trees:

1. The patient complains of left leg pain, which started this morning.
2. The patient complains of left leg pain, which started this morning when it was raining, while walking her dog uphill and after slipping in the mud.
3. The patient started having abdominal pain just after lunch today.

4. The patient started having abdominal pain just after lunch today while she was walking back to the office.

Right branching trees facilitate coherence because both the reader and writer are clear about the topic. Right branching trees give the reader a foundation on which to place new information, the qualifying information. The qualifying information builds on the foundation of the key information, which came first in the sentence.

This structure eases the mental burden on the reader because it immediately places the qualifying information into context. Right branching trees are similar to Strunk's advice to put the topic first and have successive sentences build on it.[3(p.17)] Once the writer has established the topic, the reader can *connect the dots easier*.

Left branching trees place the qualifying phrases before the foundation.[2(Ch.4)] The problem is that if you frontload the sentence with too many qualifiers, making sense of them can become more difficult.[2(Ch.4)] The reader has to keep track of the qualifiers before knowing what's being qualified.

Examples of left branching trees:
1. This morning the patient started having left leg pain.

2. This morning when it was raining, while walking her dog uphill and slipping in the mud, the patient started having left leg pain.
3. Just after lunch today, the patient started having abdominal pain.
4. Just after lunch today, while she was walking back to the office, the patient started having abdominal pain.

Left branching trees with many qualifying phrases place a greater mental burden on the reader, sometimes taking multiple reads before ascertaining the sentence's point.[2(Ch.4)] For the busy clinician, time and energy are in short supply. Understanding complicated left branching trees can be a nightmarish time drain.

Left branching trees are best used when the left branch is brief and contains few phrases.[2(Ch.4)]

Middle branching trees, which Pinker refers to as "center-embedded," are the most difficult to understand.[2(Ch.4)] The qualifiers come between the subject and the verb, distancing the action from the actor.

Examples of middle branching trees:
1. The patient, this morning, started having left leg pain.

2. The patient, who this morning in the rain while walking her dog uphill and slipping in the mud, started having left leg pain.
3. The patient, just after lunch today, started having abdominal pain.
4. The patient, just after lunch today while she was walking back to the office, started having abdominal pain.

Middle branching trees run into a similar problem as left branching trees.[2(Ch.4)] The reader must carry the burden of qualifying statements while waiting for the writer to lay the foundation. Avoid middle branching trees as much as possible.

Good Tips: Syntax
Here are a few syntactic tips that will make your charting easier for others to see your vision of the patient.

Heavier phrases go last
Put heavier, longer phrases at the end of a sentence, instead of earlier.[2(Ch.4)] Light phrases should go before heavy ones. This is similar to the concept of right branching trees. As with right branching trees, sentences with heavier phrases at the end are easier to understand.

Heavier phrase at end:
1. The chest pain was aching, heavy, left-sided, non-pleuritic, and radiating to the neck, chin and left shoulder.
2. The shortness of breath is intermittent, worse when he walks and when he lays completely flat.

Heavier phrase towards the beginning (to be avoided):
1. The chest pain was radiating towards the neck, chin and left shoulder, non-pleuritic, left sided, heavy and aching.
2. The shortness of breath is worse when he lies completely flat, when he walks, and intermittent.

<u>*Avoid 'Garden Paths': A problem of awkward syntax*</u>
Garden paths are a psycholinguistic term for ambiguous phrases with multiple, possible meanings.[2(Ch.4)] They often cause readers to backtrack and re-read in order to clarify the confusion. Garden paths do not exist in spoken language because pauses help clarify meaning.[2(Ch.4)] Punctuation is one tool to eliminate garden paths. It can take the place of the pauses and approximate the rhythm of spoken language.[2(Ch.4)] Certain pronouns can also act like punctuation to clarify garden paths, for example *that, which,* and *who*.[2(Ch.4)]

Garden path:
1. We closed the laceration with exposed muscle. (Did you close the laceration that had exposed

muscle, or did you use exposed muscle to close the laceration?)
2. I reduced the shoulder dislocation with the fractured humerus. (Was the humerus one of your tools, or was it a part of the dislocation?)

No garden path:
1. We closed the laceration that had exposed muscle.
2. I reduced the shoulder dislocation that included the fractured humerus.

Although context or a second reading can clarify their meaning, such sentences should be understood the first time and without a hint of ambiguity.

Simplify complicated sentences
Complicated sentences cloud the vision you're trying to project. How do you disentangle them? Pull unrelated phrases apart.[2(Ch.4)] Another way to think of this: *write simple sentences.*[1(p.121)]

You can even use sentence fragments when necessary.[1(p.133)] Remember that the point is to transfer your vision of the patient's story to your reader and not to maintain strict grammatical correctness. Grammar is a tool. Don't use that tool if it gets in the way.

Complicated sentences:
1. After dinner last night, the patient complained of about 4 episodes of loose, watery, non-bloody stools, as well as having crampy, intermittent, non-radiating, diffuse, abdominal pain, in addition to fever and chills.
2. Symptoms are similar to his past episodes of renal colic, which he has had intermittently for the past several years, during which the patient has hematuria, dysuria, flank pain, and intermittent urinary retention.
3. Her leg pain does not radiate, does not involve swelling, has no change in skin color, worsens when she walks, also involves numbness in all 5 toes, and differs from her chronic leg pain in that it is more intense.

Simple sentences:
1. After dinner last night, the patient had about 4 episodes of loose, watery, non-bloody stools. He also had crampy, intermittent, non-radiating, diffuse, abdominal pain. He had fever and chills.
2. Symptoms are similar to his past episodes of renal colic. He has had intermittent renal colic for several years. These symptoms include hematuria, dysuria, flank pain, and intermittent urinary retention.
3. Leg pain has no radiation, swelling or skin color change. Worsens with walking. Comes with

numbness to all toes. More intense than her chronic pain.

Voice

There are two voices in language: active and passive. The active voice focuses on someone doing something.[2(Ch.2)] The passive voice focuses on someone having something done to them.[2(Ch.2)] In other words, the passive voice directs the reader's attention away from the actor and onto the thing or person acted upon.[2(Ch.2)]

Passive:
1. The patient was brought to the emergency department by EMS.
2. I was told by the patient that [x].
3. A Coude catheter that was 18 French in size was placed by me. Straw colored urine was noted to flow easily via the tubing.
4. The area around the laceration received local anesthesia from 1% lidocaine that was injected subcutaneously by me.
5. The MRI results were discussed between the radiologist and myself.
6. The intubation of the patient was performed by the resident. This procedure was performed under my supervision.

Active:
1. EMS brought the patient to the emergency department.
2. The patient told me [x].
3. I placed an 18 French Coude catheter. Straw colored urine drained easily.
4. I achieved anesthesia around the laceration with subcutaneous 1% lidocaine.
5. The radiologist and I discussed the MRI results.
6. The resident intubated the patient. I supervised this procedure.

If the purpose of a medical chart is to transfer information about your actions to others, then be active. Use the active voice.

According to Pinker, the passive voice shows that writers have forgotten their role. Writers know the outcome and have just described it, when instead, they should be staging an event for their readers.[2(Ch.2)] A sentence in the passive voice tells. It doesn't show. Because it does not show, the passive voice can be more taxing to the reader.[2(Ch.2)] The reader must fill in the action that the writer declines to describe.

Strunk notes another advantage of the active voice: typically, it is more direct and concise.[3(p.19)] Direct and concise is usually easier to understand.

Passive voice: an occasional exception
The classic teaching from Strunk and other authors is to avoid the passive voice, [1(p.122),2(Ch.2),3(p.19)]. However, sometimes its strategic use will be a better choice.

Sometimes you may want to emphasize the object instead of the actor.

Through passive voice, you can postpone mentioning an actor that a heavy phrase describes.[2(Ch.4)] This eases the mental pressure on the reader by putting a heavier phrase towards the end.

Active:
1. The patient's wound that had a pressure dressing and that Dr. X attempted to debride yesterday drained serosanguinous fluid.
2. The bumper of the car the patient had just gotten out of struck the patient in the knee.
3. An assailant with a spatula that had just been on a hot grill caused the hand laceration.
4. Four hours of manual labor in the middle of the day that included chopping wood and digging ditches preceded the patient's collapse.

Passive (an occasional better choice):
1.   Serosanguinous fluid was draining from the wound that had a pressure dressing and that Dr. X attempted to debride yesterday.
2.   The patient's knee was struck by the bumper of the car she had just gotten out of.
3.   The hand laceration was caused by an assailant with a spatula that had just been on a hot grill.
4.   The patient's collapse was preceded by four hours of intense manual labor in the middle of the day that included chopping wood and digging ditches.

Words

The form in which thoughts occur to a writer is rarely the same as the form by which they can be absorbed by a reader.[2(Ch.3)]

Select your words carefully.

Avoid long words when shorter ones will suffice.[1(p.117)] Some writers may try to look impressive by using longer words.[1(p117)] Pinker specifically advises avoiding "fancy words you barely understand."[2(Ch.1)] This risks making the writer look pompous or even less intelligent.[2(Ch.1)] When in doubt, consider King's advice to keep the first word that comes to mind, because it is likely truer to your intent than its replacement.[1(p.118)]

With that said, remember to keep your audience in mind. Medical professionals use an industry-specific vocabulary and terminology that is unfamiliar to most non-medical people. Fancy words to non-medical people are everyday work vocabulary for medical professionals.

Use medical terminology but avoid complicating 'everyday language' in an attempt to make yourself seem impressive. The chart is not about you or your vocabulary. It is about communicating your vision of the patient's story clearly.

Plain Language is Best

The techniques and concepts that we discussed are tools to achieve the goal of writing medical charts in plain language. The website www.plainlanguage.gov sums it up this way:

> *Plain language is language your audience can understand the first time they read the prose.*[5]

Can your audience:
- Find what they need?
- Understand what they find?
- Use what they find to meet their needs?[5]

Keep in mind that no one single technique will help you achieve plain language.[5] Do not focus upon finding the 'right way' to write. Instead, use whatever helps you express your vision clearly, because in this case, the ends do justify the means. The ends or outcomes of good writing are: ease of use and understanding.[5]

Aim for the goal of plain language, and your charting should become clearer and more concise.

Show. Don't Tell.

Keep to the old advice to "Show. Don't tell." Readers understand and remember material better when descriptions are concrete, because they allow people to form visual images.[2(Ch.3)]

Remember that while you're building up evidence to support your conclusion, you're trying to draw your vision of the patient's story in words:
- Lay your evidence out and let it lead to your conclusion.

- Make your imagery specific, definite and concrete.
- Tell your writer what to see, not how to see.[3(p.21)]

King specifically advises avoiding adverbs, because adverbs show that authors suspect that they haven't expressed themselves clearly.[1(p.124)]

Telling:
1. The patient appeared sober.
2. The patient was in respiratory distress.
3. The patient was uncomfortable from abdominal pain.
4. Normal neurological exam.
5. Appears depressed.

Showing:
1. The patient had clear speech, attended to our entire conversation, cooperated throughout the entire re-assessment, had normal finger to nose bilaterally and walked the length of the ER with a stable gait.
2. Respiratory rate 28. Accessory muscle use. Speaking more than 2 words makes her short of breath.
3. The patient sat up in the stretcher, grimacing, rocking back and forth, and holding his abdomen with both hands.

4. Clear speech. Cranial nerves 2-12 within normal limits. 5/5 strength in all 4 extremities. Finger to nose normal bilaterally. Normal gait.
5. Speaks in low, monotone voice. Flat affect. Tells me he is constantly sad the past 2 weeks.

Be confident that you are painting a picture and leading the reader to your conclusion. If you lay out the key parts of your vision well enough, your readers will tend to agree with you.

Omit Unnecessary or Confusing Words

You cannot write every possible detail of the patient's story, and over-description can leave your readers lost.[1(p.174)] Balance "Show. Don't tell" with another of Strunk's classic rules: "Omit needless words."[3(p.22)]

According to psycholinguistics, interjecting a new word into a sentence poses two demands on the reader:
1. Understanding the word and
2. Fitting it into the syntax tree.[2(Ch.4)]

This requires your readers to work harder in order to understand what you have written. Mental energy and time are limited resources. Be kind to your readers by omitting unnecessary words. In the process, your vision will become clearer.

Excess words:

1. I discussed the patient's findings suspicious for bowel obstruction including increased bowel sounds, diffuse tenderness, persistent vomiting, and tympanic abdomen with on-call surgeon, Dr. X. She agrees with admission to her service for further management as an inpatient with likely non-operative management.

2. She tells me her chest pain is similar to her previous episodes of chest pain in that it is left sided, radiates to her left shoulder, has associated shortness of breath, has associated dizziness, and worsens when she walks. However, she also tells me that it is more intense than her previous episodes and walking triggers it more easily. Given these, changes will admit of suspected acute coronary syndrome.

3. The patient had a fall while trying to walk to the bathroom. His nurse informed me that he fell. I went to the bedside to perform an evaluation of him. He told me he did not want to ask the nurse to assist him in walking to the bathroom. He denied LOC and pain, but had trouble standing. His face and scalp had no lacerations, abrasions, swelling or bruising. His extremities had full range of motion, no tenderness, and no swelling. I will order walker and physical therapy evaluation.

Omitting words:

1. I discussed likely small bowel obstruction with on-call surgeon, Dr. X. She agrees with admission.
2. Chest pain similar to past pain: left sided, radiates to left shoulder, SOB, dizzy, worsens when she walks. More intense and easily triggered with walking. Will admit for suspected acute coronary syndrome.
3. Fell walking to the bathroom. Told me he did not want to ask for help to the bathroom. No LOC or pain. Face and scalp: no lacerations, abrasions, swelling, bruising. All extremities: full range of motion, no tenderness, no swelling. Will order walker and physical therapy.

At the same time, you can overdo omitting words to the point of confusion. Take care in cutting out too many words.[2(Ch.4)] An occasional redundant word may keep the reader on the right path and make the meaning of a sentence easier to understand.

Over-omitted words:

1. Discussed with on-call. *(Discussed what? With whom? Why?)*

2. Chest pain worse. Admit. *(What type of chest pain? How much worse?)*
3. Fell. No serious trauma. Walker and PT. *(Where? What type of trauma? Why was a walker and PT needed?)*

In each of these cases, the patient's story in incomplete.

Good Tips: Words

Here are a few tips about word choice that will make your charting more concise and clear.

Avoid iterating conclusions

If you have been clear enough in laying out your vision, why recount every detail again that led to your conclusion? If you have truly transferred your vision into words, your reader will likely reach the conclusion before you state it.

If the information is clearly stated elsewhere, such statements at the end of your charting are redundant:

1. The history is inconsistent with small bowel obstruction because there is no vomiting, the patient is having normal bowel movements, the abdomen is non-distended and bowel sounds are not hyperactive.

2. I do not think the patient has acute coronary syndrome because the chest pain is right sided, non-exertional, non-radiating, is momentary, has no associated shortness of breath and worsens only when the patient adducts her right arm.

3. There are no clinical signs of end organ damage from hypertension as the patient does not have headache, dizziness, chest pain, or shortness of breath

If your evidence has already been clearly stated, then just state your conclusion:

1. The findings are inconsistent with small bowel obstruction.

2. My assessment of the patient's clinical picture shows no signs of coronary artery disease.

3. The patient has no clinical signs of end organ damage from hypertension.

Avoid Multiple Negatives
Multiple negatives leads to more mental work and confusion for your readers.[2(Ch.5)] More than the traditional double negative, the issue of multiple negatives includes negative words, such as:
- Few,

- Little,
- Least,
- Seldom,
- Though,
- Rarely,
- Instead,
- Doubt,
- Deny,
- Refute,
- Avoid, and
- Ignore.[2(Ch.5)]

Too many negatives confuse the wording of the sentence and may actually create the opposite of the writer's intention. Positive descriptions and assertions are easier to understand.[2(Ch.5)]

Multiple negatives:
1. No abnormal findings.
2. The patient does not rarely have these symptoms.
3. The family told me the patient's complaints are not unusual for her under these circumstances.
4. He tells me he never does not have back pain.

Positive:
1. Normal exam. (Better yet, specify what you examined)
2. The patient has these symptoms often. (Better yet, specify the frequency)

3. The family told me the patient's complaints are typical for her under these circumstances.
4. He tells me he always has back pain.

Save yourself and your reader unnecessary time and energy. Omit needless words.

Writing A Legal Document

Physicians clearly see how their charts can be used as a bill and a form of clinical information transfer, but many are unfamiliar with the medical chart's precise role in the medical malpractice system. Your chart is a legal document. In the case of a malpractice suit, your chart will be a central part of your defense.

To understand how to chart effectively as a legal document, we will dedicate some time and space to context. This will include a brief overview of the American medical malpractice system, since it is unfamiliar to many physicians. Our discussion will also include the experience, and costs of medical malpractice for physicians.

Context: Medical Malpractice in the United States

Medical malpractice is a centuries-old phenomenon. American medical malpractice comes from the English legal tradition, when as early as the 1300s, cases included discussions of fault and standard of care.[6] By the 1830s in the United States, medical malpractice had reached crisis levels.[6] Over the following decades, the law has swung back and forth between defense-friendly and plaintiff-friendly.[6]

The American Medical Malpractice Process

The American judicial system is adversarial in that the plaintiff and the defense advocate for their respective sides with well-reasoned arguments. This is supposed to lead to better decisions.[7]

The general process is as follows:

First, the allegedly injured patient, or his or her estate, files a complaint. This complaint alleges medical negligence in the patient's treatment. There are 4 elements of medical negligence, and the plaintiff must prove all four elements in order to demonstrate medical negligence:

1. The physician owes a duty to treat the patient.
2. The treatment fell below standard of care.
3. Failure of medical treatment caused injury to the patient.
4. Damages directly resulted from breach of standard of care.[8]

The defendant physician or a representative receives the complaint and then must respond to the allegations. Typically, the physician's defense attorney makes the response.

If the defense response is that there was no malpractice, the next stage is <u>discovery</u>; both sides gather evidence about the case. Gathering evidence includes obtaining medical charts, finding medical experts, and taking depositions. Depositions are interviews wherein attorneys question witnesses without the supervision of a judge. Depositions are sworn testimony.

The next step is a <u>jury trial</u>. The judge acts as a referee to make sure that both the defense and the plaintiff follow proper procedures. The jury is the trier of fact, the ultimate decider of the case. During the trial, attorneys on both sides have the opportunity to present their side of the case to the jury.

At any point in this process: <u>the case may settle</u>. Either side may initiate a settlement. The defense may be able to negotiate terms that the plaintiff finds agreeable. Alternatively, the plaintiff may decide not to pursue the case further.

**Medical Malpractice Outcomes: Physicians'
Experiences and Costs**

The consequences of medical malpractice trouble physicians, despite the fact that the system generally favors them:
- Courts dismiss just over half of claims.[9]

- 80% of the cases that go to jury trial result in the physician winning.[9]

When a physician loses, monetary rewards rarely exceed the limits of the insurance policy.[6,] Nevertheless, I have seen physicians literally trembling at the mere thought of being involved in a medical malpractice suit.

Medical malpractice is a time-consuming and expensive job hazard. A 2013 Medscape survey of physicians across multiple specialties noted that:

- More than 25% spent more than 40 hours helping prepare for their defense.[10]
- Just over 25% who went to trial reported spending more than 40 hours for trial and trial-related meetings alone. [10]
- Almost 60% described the whole process as lasting between 1-5 years.[10]

Even when physicians win their cases, they've spent considerable time, spent considerable energy, and lost money in potential earnings. [10]

There are also significant emotional and psychological costs. The same survey highlighted how traumatic the charge of medical malpractice can be. [10] Almost 40% of physician respondents rated the experience as either "horrible: one of the worst experiences of my life" or "very bad: disruptive and humiliating." [10] Physicians can feel hurt or angry when a person whom they tried their best to help later accuses them of malpractice.[11]

They also may fear the loss of control, livelihood, assets, and reputation.[11]

During this process, a physician may suffer from *Medical Malpractice Litigation Stress Syndrome*.[11] Symptoms include anxiety, irritability, shame, loneliness, lack of focus, emotional distancing, and substance abuse.[11] This syndrome can lead to burnout, physical illness, early retirement, and suicide.[11]

Good charting plays an important role in minimizing the risk of malpractice.

How Good Charting Helps the Physician, Medico-Legally

Revisiting 'Defensive Charting': Is it good charting?

Defensive charting is an extension of defensive medical practice. Defensive medical practice focuses solely on protecting the provider from litigation.[12] But is defensive charting good charting? Most likely not.

In "Fear of Malpractice Liability and its Role in Clinical Decision Making," Hauser *et al.* make a distinction between defensive charting and quality charting.[12] Defensive documentation typically:

- Has physicians put too many details into the chart,

- Is time consuming, and
- Moves the focus away from quality charting.[12]

In contrast, quality charting focuses on:

- Pertinent details, and
- Decision-making.[12]

Quality charting echoes the advice for good writing that we have already discussed.[1,3,4]

Clear transfer of your vision is the same for both the medico-legal and clinical communication aspects of the chart:

1. Make your vision clear,
2. Make your audience agree with what you did, and
3. Make clear why your course of action was a reasonable one, at the time.

Expert Witnesses and Medical Charts

Let's return to an important concept that we discussed earlier: *Know your audience.*

A key member of a medical malpractice audience is the expert medical witness. Expert witnesses are typically physicians in the same specialty as the accused. Their tasks are to review the medical record, apply their medical expertise, and provide a professional opinion on questions, such as:

- Was there a breach in standard of care?
- Did the damages result from the breach in standard of care?
- Did the treating physician miss the diagnosis?

Convincing expert witnesses of your vision will go a long way towards defending your decisions. Although expert witnesses are only one part of the greater medical malpractice process, they play an important part at key points.

To illustrate, let's consider a question of standard of care, and the role of the medical chart. In general, standard of care is determined by what a similarly trained physician in a similar circumstance would do. Shortly after the allegedly injured patient contacts an attorney, the attorney will typically hire a medical expert to verify the merits of the case. The plaintiff expert will then review the chart and give the plaintiff attorney his or her opinion. A chart may convince the plaintiff expert that treatment met standard of care if it:

1. Clearly transfers the accused physician's vision to the expert witness' mind,
2. Shows how the accused physician's decisions logically followed that vision.

If the plaintiff's expert says that the accused physician met standard of care, this indicates to the plaintiff's attorney that the case has no merit and the case might not be filed at all.

If the plaintiff expert finds that the treatment was below standard of care, then the plaintiff attorney files the complaint. The defense attorney will hire his or her own expert. This expert will typically also be in the same specialty as the accused. The defense expert will also review the chart.

If the defense expert also reports that treatment was indeed below standard of care, then the defense attorney is likely to settle. However, if the chart convinces the defense expert that treatment met standard of care, then the defense attorney will typically recommend fighting the case.

When both sides have valid arguments, then the result can go either way. Legal proceedings will then include a battle of the experts.

What can stop the plaintiff expert from claiming that treatment was below standard of care, even when treatment had met standard of care? Two things:
    1. A defense expert, and
    2. Their own reputation.

A blatantly incorrect expert opinion will be easy for the other side to discredit.

Reputation is important in both the legal and expert witness industries. No one wants to be on the losing side. Clients do not want lawyers who lose, and lawyers do not want experts who helped other lawyers lose.

The extent to which your chart:
- Reflects your vision of the patient's situation, and
- Demonstrates how your decisions followed logically

will help decide whether part of the process swings towards or against your favor. Even if you are ultimately clinically wrong, you will be judged on what you did with what you knew at the time.

If you convince medical experts of your vision with the evidence you provide, then your well-written chart will have done its job. A well-written chart that clearly shows your vision of the patient's situation will:
1. Give your defense expert more tools to work with,
2. Give the plaintiff expert less to work with, and
3. May even convince the plaintiff expert that the accusations have no merit.

Insights from Expert Witnesses

In her article, "Medical Charting Errors Can Drive Patient Liability Suits," Gallegos interviewed medical malpractice defense attorneys and identified common charting problems cited against providers:
1. Incomplete charts,
2. No documented communication with staff and other providers, and
3. Copying and pasting, especially from one chart to another.[13]

She further advised charting discussions with patients.[13]

I conducted my own survey of medical expert witnesses, asking them to list common problems that they found in their medical chart reviews. The most common involved:

Pre-populated templates
Templates become a problem when inconsistent with information in the rest of the chart. For example:
- Template states that there were normal cranial nerves 2-12, but the rest of the chart suggests a stroke with facial droop.
- Template states there is no fever, but the clearly documented vital signs indicate otherwise.

The discrepancy breaks the coherence of the vision and the patient's story, posing questions for reliability, credibility, and accuracy:

1. *What should the reader believe when the template section of the chart contradicts the free text portion?*
2. *How reliable is the rest of the chart?*

When the discrepancy is integral to the case at hand, the discrepancy can destroy the chart's defensibility.
Be as thoughtful in editing your template as you are in writing the prose in your chart.

Being too brief
Remember over-omitting needless words? Sometimes, physicians omit necessary ones, rendering the chart useless. If your details are too sparse:

- You're not painting your picture of the patient's story, and
- You're not giving your readers enough information to re-create your vision accurately.

Strike the balance between eliminating useless words and telling the story.

Balancing the Curse of Knowledge with over-description is probably one of the most difficult tasks when charting. **Try to take the perspective of an outside reader.**

Lack of focus
Focus on the problem at hand. Be thorough about the central issue. Remember to include the pertinent details.[1(p.173),3(p.22),4(Ch.4)] Beware of extraneous details that

distract from your picture of the patient's central problem.
Tell only one central story.

Differential diagnosis
Make sure your differential diagnosis is complete. Address each item of that diagnosis. If you have subarachnoid hemorrhage on your written differential diagnosis list, then be sure that you address this possibility with your actions in the chart.
Follow through and document.

Abnormal results
Make sure the results match your exam findings. The different pieces of the story should fit into the vision you are drawing.
Address all abnormal results.

Clinical reasoning
When necessary, spell out your reasoning:
- Why did you do what you did?
- Why are certain items in your differential diagnosis unlikely?

Demonstrate your thought process.

Discussions
Include not only what was discussed, but also who was there.

- Who did you speak to? Was it the patient, the spouse, a sibling, a parent, a neighbor, etc?
- Who was there during follow-up discussions or discharge?

Knowing who was there and what was said becomes important when people are called as trial witnesses.

Reassessments

Reassessments tell your vision of the patient's story, since they may explain your actions and motives.

For example, charting a patient with an asthma exacerbation, drawing a picture of a mild exacerbation, making an initial plan of discharge home, and then having the next documentation be a crash tracheostomy will raise a lot of questions.

Document all reassessments.

Discharge instructions

Make sure discharge instructions are clear and easy to understand. Patients should know:

- What to expect,
- What to do for self-care, and
- Under which circumstances they should seek medical attention.

Well-written discharge instructions put some of the responsibility for healthcare back onto the patient.

Nursing notes

Address the nursing note, if inconsistencies exist.

Failure to do so raises suspicion that you ignored or missed potentially vital information.

Avoid these potentially costly mistakes early on by cultivating good charting habits now.

A Note about Electronic Charting Systems

Many modern electronic charting systems allow their users to use templates and functions, such as copy and paste. Although these tools are meant to save time, they can be pitfalls. Remember,
These tools can increase the risk of inconsistencies:
- *Within your chart, and*
- *Between the chart and what actually happened.*

If you're going to use templates, use them with the same care that you use in writing your own prose.
Make sure you tell a consistent story with a clear vision throughout the entire chart.

<u>Conclusion</u>

Charting takes time, whether it's dictated, electronic or on paper. As clinicians, the thrust of our jobs is caring for patients. Documentation is only one of several responsibilities. It can be time consuming, and our time is limited. However, you must balance the time-crunch with telling the patient's story in a logical and complete manner.

1. **Avoid needless repetition.** Needless repetition can put additional mental burden on the readers and get them lost. Repeating yourself unnecessarily also wastes time. Say what you have to say once, and say it well. If you repeat yourself, do it consciously, and do it to emphasize an important point.

2. **Try to read your chart at least once before you consider it finished**. While you are doing this, ask yourself the following:
   - *Does this chart show the vision of the patient's story as I see it?*
   - *Would an outside reader in your specialty read my chart and agree with me?*

3. **Re-evaluate your thought process regarding the patient's story**, if you find that something does not fit that vision, and the culprit is not the writing. Your initial vision of the patient's story may be wrong.

It's ok if this happens. While writing is refined thinking, writing also *refines* your thinking. Your writing may lead you to an alternate diagnosis or treatment plan.

Many tools exist for writers to express themselves. I've introduced only a few of them in this book. Whatever tools you decide to use, keep in mind the concept of writing in plain language:

Is your writing easy to use, easy to understand and easy to read?[5]

Remember the ultimate goal is clear communication of your vision.

Like the practice of medicine, writing is a continuous process of learning and growing. Good, clear, efficient written communication is a journey, not a destination. It can be a life-long journey, if you let it.

Good luck.

<u>Acknowledgements</u>

Without the following people, I would not have been
able to make this book a reality.

I want to give a special thanks to:

Antonio Mendez, MD, JD

Tamara Fish

Tanya Pohl, JD

Wallace Carter, MD

Endnotes

1. Stephen King. *On Writing – A Memoir of the Craft* (New York, NY: Scribner, 2000).
2. Stephen Pinker. *The Sense of Style* (New York, NY: Penguin Group, 2014).
3. William Strunk Jr. and E. B. White. *The Elements of Style, 4th ed.* (New York, NY: Longman, 1999).
4. Stanley Fish. *How to Write a Sentence and How to Read One* (New York, NY: Harper-Collins, 2011).
5. What is plain language? Plainlanguage.gov website. http://www.plainlanguage.gov/whatisPL/ Accessed 1/15/2015.
6. Bucker F. American medical malpratice. In: Sanbar S, ed. *The Medical Malpractice Survival Handbook.* Philadelphia: Moby Elsevier; 2007: 3-8.
7. Sanbar S. The American court system. In: Sanbar S, ed. *The Medical Malpractice Survival Handbook.* Philadelphia PA: Moby Elsevier; 2007: 221-229.
8. Sanbar S. Malpractice lawsuits: prevention, initial handling and physician concerns. In: Sanbar S, ed. *The Medical Malpractice Survival Handbook.* Philadelphia PA: Moby Elsevier; 2007: 17-28
9. Jena A, Chandra A, Lakdawalla D, Seabury S. Outcomes of medical malpractice litigation against US physicians. *Arch Intern Med*, v.17, no.11(2012):892-894.

10. Kane L. Medscape. Malpractice report: the experience of getting sued. Medscape website. July 24, 2013. http://www.medscape.com/features/slideshow/ malpractice-report/public. Accessed: 1/15/2015.
11. Sanbar S. Medical malpractice stress syndrome. In: Sanbar S, ed. *The Medical Malpractice Survival Handbook.* Philadelphia PA: Moby Elsevier; 2007: 9-16.
12. Hauser MJ, Commons ML, Bursztajn HJ, Gutheil TG. Fear of malpractice liability and its role in clinical decision making. In: Gutheil TG, Bursztajn HJ, Brodsky A, Alexander, V, eds. *Decision Making in Psychiatry and the Law*, ed. Baltimore: Williams & Wilkins, 1991.
13. Gallegos A. Medical charting errors can drive patient liability suits. www.amednews.com. March 25, 2013. http://www.amednews.com/article/20130325/pro fession/130329979/5/. Accessed 1/15/2015.

Appendix: The Original 2 Page Handout

A few tips on charting...

A medical chart is many things. It serves legal, medical communication and billing functions. Legally, it may be your **only** defense. Medically, the chart transfers information to another healthcare provider who will take care of the patient in the future. For billing, your chart is the proof of your work and a kind of **RECEIPT.**

Much like a manual laborer who is paid more if more bags are moved or more holes are dug, we (or our hospital) are compensated more for doing more work. In healthcare, this usually equates to mental work. More complex cases translate to more mental work. We demonstrate this in a medical chart.

In a sense, the core of our jobs is to gather information, synthesize it into a cohesive picture and make decisions based upon the result of this process. Your chart should reflect this.

Although this may not directly affect your re-imbursement as a resident, "attendinghood" is coming sooner than you realize. Remember, in many practice settings, your pay (or bonus) will be directly related to your ability to bill for services.

Re-read your chart after you are finished writing it. Make sure that it is easy to follow, cohesive, COMPLETE, and **says what you want it to say.**

Remember, you are trying to tell a STORY. Or in another sense, you are trying to build a case for why you did what you did.

History of Presenting Illness:

The more PERTINENT information you provide the better. One of the easier examples is pain.

Listing the location, duration, intensity, quality, timing, exacerbating and relieving factors of pain gives you a lot of information.

Review of Systems:

Place the other information you have gathered that does not easily fit into the HPI narrative here. The more systems you cover, the more information you have gathered, showing how much more complex the case was.

Be careful to not have this contradict your HPI.

Medical/Surgical/Social History:

How sick was this patient before they came to you? A patient with more comorbidities or social problems maybe in need of more help, more complicated and potentially requires more mental work.

Physical Exam:

How many organ systems have you really examined, formally or otherwise? Be specific as possible with your abnormalities.

The chest was tender? Ok, which side? At the level of which rib?

Medical Decision Making(AKA What I Was Thinking AKA Why I Did What I Did):

List your differential diagnosis (again proving the complexity of the case).

List your plan for addressing your differential.

Interpret your lab results (at least pick out what was significantly abnormal).

Interpret your radiology results.

FULLY interpret your EKG.

Document AS MANY DIAGNOSES AS THE PATIENT ACTUALLY HAS

Clinical Course (Re-assessment):

Pertinent details of the course go here. This often is related to "Why I Did What I Did".

Examples:

PMD contacted and requests admission to her service.

Called PMD 3 times without response. Will admit to on-call service.

Surgery consult contacted.

Neurology requests admission to medical floor.

Started antibiotics for healthcare associated pneumonia.

Patient appears better and ambulated to bathroom.

Patient became hypotensive and dopamine initiated.

Patient admitted to surgical service.

Critical Care Time:

Add this if the patient is gravely ill, has a very high chance of decompensation or required your undivided attention.

Made in the USA
Lexington, KY
10 September 2019